Stimulating Poetry II

Paul E. Crowl

Exposition Press   *Hicksville, New York*

First Edition

© 1979 by Paul E. Crowl

All rights reserved, including the right of reproduction in whole or in part, in any form or by any means, electronic or mechanical, including photocopying, recording, or by any information storage and retrieval system. No part of this book may be reproduced without permission in writing from the publisher. Inquiries should be addressed to Exposition Press, Inc., 900 South Oyster Bay Road, Hicksville, N.Y. 11801.

ISBN 0-682-49291-4

Printed in the United States of America

STIMULATING POETRY II

Paul E. Crowl
1981

Paul E. Crowl
16707 Marygold, #801
Fontana, CA 92335

*To my son and his family,
and all of the many people
who helped to inspire me*

Contents

Preface	9
Kindergartners	13
Alone	14
We Care	15
Never Alone	15
Grand View Baptist Church	16
Into the Sunset	17
The Artist	18
A Piece of Clay	19
In the Shadows	20
Reminiscing	20
Reminiscences	21
When Heaven Seemed So Near	22
Retirement	22
When I Retire	23
I Believe	24
The Wind	25
Security	26
The Santana Winds	27
A Warning	28
Maine	29
Arizona	30
Idaho	31
The City	32
Thought	33
Live	34
The One-Room School	35
To Mandy	36
To Vega (in Sweden)	37
Why I Love You	40

To Vega	40
Love	41
Cooled Love	42
A Fling	43
Deadly Game	44
The Beach	45
Grin and Bear It	46
To My Friends	47
Poetry	48
Autumn	49
Awaiting His Call	50
Church	51
Old Age	52
An Ode to a Timeworn Heart	53
Glendora	54
The Foothills	55
The San Gabriel Valley Symphony	56
Memories	57
Stress	58
Is God Dead?	59
Today I'm Sixty	60
Announcement	61
Our Baby	62
Spring	63
Milestones	64
Endearments	65
The Astronauts	71
From One Republican to Another	72
Utopia	73
Complaints	74
The Pirates	75
Christmas	76
A Christmas to Remember	77
A Christmas Thought	78
My Thrill	79

Preface

The purpose of this book is to bring together a collection of my poetry, done over a period of sixty years, for the pleasure and enjoyment of all who read it.

While writing these lines it was not my intention to have them published. They were a source of pleasure and enjoyment—to be reread in my leisure—helping me to relive the pleasant moments I had, not only in writing them, but in the situations that were the inspiration of each of them.

Now that I have published them, it is my hope that you as a reader will enjoy them also. Perhaps one of them will awaken some memory of your early years, or bring back a tender thought, or, perhaps, help you to spend a few quiet moments just thinking.

STIMULATING POETRY II

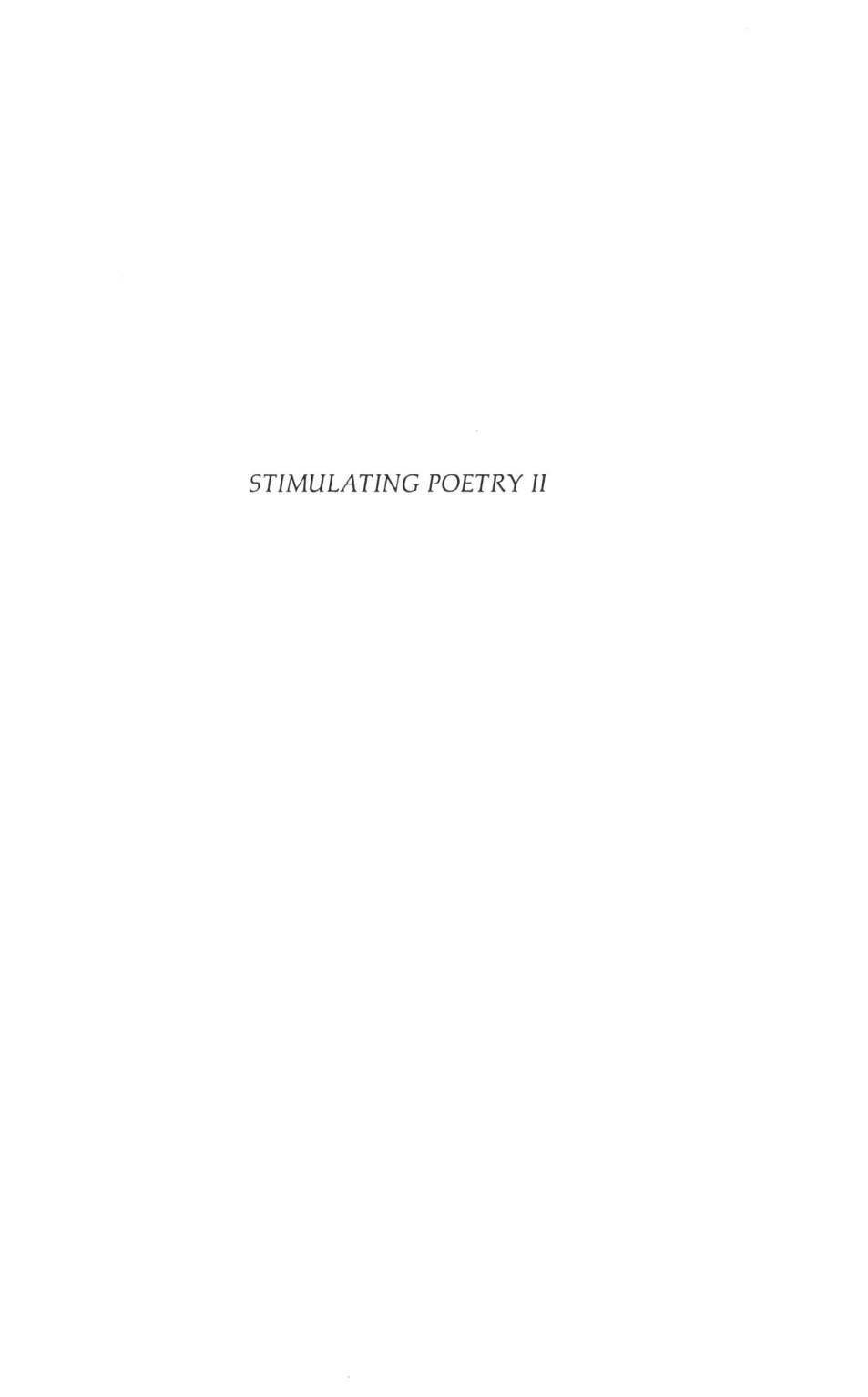

Kindergartners

Little girls and little boys,
At last you're here in class
To learn the many, many things,
So that each year you'll pass.
Don't be afraid and never cry,
For we'll have loads of fun,
Playing games like big kids do
And meeting everyone.
Then soon we'll learn the ABCs,
So we can learn to spell.
Numbers are another game
That you'll enjoy quite well.
And then when you grow really tired,
And want to sit and rest,
We all will close our tiny eyes—
We know we've done our best.
Perhaps we'll dream a little bit
Of As and Bs and Cs
And all the numbers that we know,
Like 1s and 2s and 3s.

Alone

People never are alone,
If they would stop and think
Of all the places they have been
And all the folks they've met,
Or close their eyes, perchance, and
Dream of things that will come yet.

People never are alone,
If they will only smile,
And as they walk along the street,
Or travel in a car,
They nod to those who pass them by,
And be just what they are.

Some folks are lonely in a crowd
And don't join in the fun.
They stand and wait for someone else
To take them by the hand.
But if they radiate their love,
They'll find they're in demand.

We Care

The reason for my being here,
Is warmth, understanding, and to be near
To others with a need like mine;
To guide me through the lonely time;
To meet and greet somebody new,
Someone to tell my troubles to,
Someone to touch, someone to share,
Or seek advice from someone there;
But, most of all, when meetings close
The HUGS one gets before one goes.

Never Alone

The beauty of a summer's day,
The warmth of sunshine in the air,
The fragrance of the flowers in bloom,
Around us everywhere.

The moonlight of a winter's night,
Bathing all in silvery glow,
Eerie shadows cross our path,
Tiny flakes of falling snow.

All are there for us to see,
Each a wonder of its own;
No one ever need to be
Lonely or alone.

Grand View Baptist Church

Dropping in to a church, at the top of the Mount,
In the rain and the low-hanging clouds,
I could not but think that not long ago
Christ stood on a Mount and preached to a crowd.

As I entered the door, I felt not alone,
For I was greeted with much warmth and love.
A beautiful feeling encompassed me there,
For, I know, He watched down from above.

All through the service, I could see in the faces
Joy and happiness banished their cares.
The Choir and the Solo so brilliantly done,
The Hymns had a radiant air.

At last I have found a church of renown;
They know what Religion's about.
Tho I was just passing through, I will never forget
That church on the top of the Mount.

Into the Sunset

As I drove down the highway this evening,
The sun, a huge ball in the sky,
Clouds with their gold and red highlights,
Enjoying their last hour's good-bye,
A sadness in all of the brilliance,
For a beautiful day is now o'er,
And soon there will be only darkness,
And the beauty so loved is no more.
Life has a way of reflecting
The joys of a wonderful day;
In our hearts and our minds we will cherish
Those moments so worthwhile that stay.
Like friendship, tho oft hard to come by,
And acquaintances, like grains of sand, are
Around us each day at our elbow,
But scarcely they offer a hand,
Love we must not take too lightly.
It's so complex; it's hard to define.
Ofttimes we misquote it, for fondness,
Or companionship, some of the time.
Let not our hearts be too troubled,
For God in His way seems to know
That which is best for His children,
Guiding them on as they go.
And so as the sunset grows dimmer,
And brightness now turns into shade,
Remember that life too has its brilliance,
Before it sinks down in the glade.

The Artist

Man cannot live and work each day,
Without a little bit of play.
Give him a palette, brush, and paint.
Though his efforts may be faint,
He'll be a better man.

He'll see new colors, tones, and hues,
And many things he never knew.
The trees, the grass, the clouded sky,
And all the things he once passed by
Will mean much more to him.

He'll take a new aspect on life,
Forgetting pain and aches and strife.
He'll see the grandeur all around;
A richer life will then abound,
And he will live again.

A Piece of Clay

Only a shapeless piece of clay,
Clammy, cold, forlorn,
Yet skillful hands of a craftsman
Will give it shape and form.

Combining love and patience,
Ingenuity, sweat, and tears,
Finally, from that piece of clay,
A work of art appears.

A warm and shapely figurine,
So beautiful and gay,
It seems to live and offers joy
To all who come that way.

In the Shadows

Each hour, each day, another year,
We wait in sunset's final rays.
Yesterday we loved and sang and fully lived;
Today is just another passing day.
Tomorrow, who will know, for we may never greet the
    dawn;
Yet here we sit, peaceful, sad, forlorn, but calm.

Reminiscing

We do not mourn our passing;
Our years were rich and full of joy and life.
Too bad we cannot will the knowledge that we gained,
To save this world from future bitterness and strife.

Reminiscences

When I look back to long ago,
Then we were family, as you know,
We did the things all families do—
But that has changed; those days are through.

As years go by and times change too,
You have your life, but mine's most through.
I cherish all those times we had,
When we could laugh and be so glad.

The holidays, the trips we took,
The picnics by the babbling brook,
The birthday parties every year,
The shopping sprees, and Christmas cheer.

All this is gone, but I don't mind;
I lived my time and now I find
Peace and contentment every day,
As I slowly while my life away.

When Heaven Seemed So Near

On Bluebird Hill among the stars,
Where fragrance fills the air,
And one looks down on myriad lights,
All their beauty to share.

A feeling stirred within my heart,
For heaven seemed so near,
As though I could reach out and grasp,
The things we hold so dear.

Angelic music, soft and sweet,
Mere words cannot express
The gratitude I felt last night,
Midst all the happiness.

Retirement

Some years ago, when I was young,
  And full of pep and vigor,
I wondered just what it was like
To be retired and loaf and rest.
But now that time is really here,
I'm not too sure it's for the best.

I'm still too young, in many ways,
  To lead an idle life.
And doing nothing is a bore,
For there's so many things to do.
Guess I'll start a newfound fad
And start life all anew.

When I Retire

How many times, how often said,
"When I myself retire,
I'm going to travel far and wide;
A nomad then I'll be.
I'll see the mountains and the plains;
I'll go from sea to sea."

I want to see the other side,
When I myself retire,
The places far away from here,
Away from noise and din,
Where I can stretch my arms and see
What beauty lies within.

I want to see the tallest peaks,
When I myself retire,
And fish the streams, untouched by man,
Or bask beneath a tree,
And drink the beauty all about,
My naked eye can see.

And then when I have seen it all,
When I myself retire,
I'll have a storehouse filled with dreams,
That always can be used
To drive away those lonely hours,
And keep me well amused.

I Believe

I believe that everyone in this wide world,
Will be just what God wanted them to be.
We all are given bodies, minds, and souls;
We all have equal opportunity.

We see the sky, the stars, the sun, and moon;
We breathe the air and feel the glow of life.
And all of nature's beauty we enjoy
Without a thought of bitterness or strife.

The greed and hate that festers in our hearts
Is caused by man, and man alone can change.
Who dares to say that "they are all divine,"
When only one has ever reached that range.

Our race and creed and color of our skin
Are only ways of telling where we dwell.
Were we to live as one, in just one place,
Time would erase this means by which we tell.

Do unto others that which you want them to do;
Covet not the gain or fortunes others hold.
Seek to better that which tends to be your lot;
Remember, all that glitters is not gold.

The Wind

Out from the desert, into the sun,
First like a whisper it comes,
Rustling the leaves on the tips of trees,
Cooling the brow of each one.

Then about four, it comes with a roar,
Gusts shaking valley and glen.
At hurricane force, it drives down its course,
To the ocean to return again.

Skies become clear; smog is all gone,
A beautiful California day,
Kissed by the sun, days filled with fun,
Now that the wind is away.

Security

Here I sit in my humble abode,
While the rain outside beats on the roof,
Snug and warm in my easy chair,
Feeling secure and highly aloof.

Then to my mind a thought appears;
'Twas only yesterday that tragedy struck.
Now all those souls, who felt as I,
Are deep enmeshed in mud and muck.

First, 'twas but a winter rain,
Then, all at once, the clouds did part.
The downfall rivaled Noah's flood;
Chaos reigned, once it did start.

Homes and buildings, there they stood,
A monument to a builder's dream.
Now, torn and battered, filled with mud,
They lay beside the rushing stream.

No one should be as snug as I,
For God can change the image, when
He feels that we are too secure
And have no further need of Him.

The Santana Winds

The hot wind blows o'er sandy dunes,
Parched, wrinkled leaves cry out from thirst.
The busy workman swabs his sweaty brow,
The farmer, always fearing for the worst.

Strong zephyrs off the burning sands,
Those scorching, searing, hated winds,
Bringing tension, anger, hate, and thirst,
To an already turmoiled land within.

Cooling fans, seeded clouds, angry words,
Nothing seems to stem the burning flow,
Crying babies, sullen children, listless parents,
The hated season when Santana winds do blow.

A Warning

The greatest nation in the world
With beauty unsurpassed,
With riches, strength, and modern skills,
With holdings far and vast.

More powerful than all before,
More skilled in craft and art,
Yet through this empire there is found
A weakness in its heart.

The love of man does not exist;
Corruption's far and wide,
Lust for power in politics,
And morals cast aside.

Fiendish crimes, we tolerate;
Vice is everywhere,
So busy in our quest for wealth,
That no one seems to care.

We now are at the peak of time,
When we should stop and think,
For history points out many things,
And we stand on the brink.

Maine

A sturdy home on sturdy ground,
Buildings, built to last and last,
A state where freedom first was found,
And rugged souls were cast.

Cloud-kissed skies so clear and blue,
Storm-tossed seas, where ships remain,
A monument to those souls we knew,
Who lived and died for Maine.

Lobsters, treats fit for a King,
Oysters from the briny deep,
Here we have most everything,
Farms and factories for our keep.

Winter snows, maple time,
Sleigh and church bells peal their song,
As o'er the vales and hills we climb,
Happy as we ride along.

This is the land that God has blessed,
The background of this nation,
Where love of liberty had its test
And freedom's celebration.

Arizona

Arizona's golden sun and azure sky,
So clean and clear and blue,
A land to live in, a land to love,
A land of plenty, too.

A place where sky meets fertile land,
Where shades and hues abound,
Framing a portrait, a masterpiece,
Of beauty all around.

Fantastic cliffs shaped by the wind,
And rain and sun and sand,
Gold and silver here are found,
Awaiting the seeking hand.

Cotton, corn, and other grains,
Rich in the good from the earth,
Water to quench the thirsty soil,
And give new growth rebirth.

This is home to the Navajo,
Where Indian lore holds sway.
It's also home to the white man,
Whose progress is here to stay.

A fortunate place to settle,
A beautiful place to be,
A place where life is worth living,
In the arms of God's luxury.

Idaho

Each night I lie awake and dream
Of places far away.

Of mountains towering to the sky,
Of sloping hills and meadows green,
And wish that I might someday go
To that great State of Idaho.

My fondest wish when I retire
And have much time to spare,
To see the trees and rushing streams,
To fish for trout and hunt the deer,
Enjoying nature as I go
In that great State of Idaho.

To breathe the air so sweet and clean,
See beauty unsurpassed,
The shrouded spires, so glistening white,
The smell of wood smoke in the breeze,
The crackling frost and winter's snow
In that great State of Idaho.

The City

Lofty buildings, dirty streets, dark alleys,
Human misery, suffering, disease, starvation,
Strained laughter, screams, anguished cries,
Cooking smells, garbage, filthy sanitation.

Painted women, bearded men, dirty children,
Battered cars, trash, decayed vegetation.
Vermin, dogs, and felines on the prowl,
Filthy streets, shabby flats, human resignation.

Thought

The gates were closed on me one day,
A prisoner of the State,
The friends and pleasures I once had,
The thrill of freedom I once knew—
Remembered all too late.
With cold bleak walls on every side,
A prison life to face,
Guards to watch my every move,
All privileges for me are gone—
The shame and the disgrace.
Each day, a year torn from my life,
Could fate have set the stage
That sent me out that terrible night
To do the deed that brought me here
And filled my heart with rage?
Why did I make that great mistake
And lose what I had prized?
God, give me strength to make amends.
Just one more chance is all I ask,
For now I realize.
Here life has changed my way of thought;
All bitterness is past.
With daily work and studies, too,
New views and hopes are mine,
For I can plan ahead at last,
When that day comes and I am free,
To face the world anew.
The knowledge I have gained while here,
The attitude that I now have,
Will help to see me through.

Live

So live your life that when you die,
You leave behind a better world.
And all the efforts that you gave
Will live and last beyond the grave.

For every day while you are here,
Before you say that last good-bye,
Help someone else to find his way,
Then you'll enjoy a brighter day.

Covet not another's gain;
Be satisfied with what you have.
Enrich yourself with what you give,
By teaching others how to live.

Wear a smile, a pleasant face;
Radiate your happiness.
It's contagious, you will find,
If you keep this thought in mind.

When that day does finally come,
And they lay you out to rest,
Worry not to where you go;
You and God will only know.

The One-Room School

Although it's been a long, long time,
Since we have been in touch,
I still remember the One-Room School
And the Teacher I liked so much.

Those were the times, when hearts were young,
And stars were in our eyes.
Those were the days that meant so much
In fashioning later lives.

I'm thankful for that One-Room School
And the pleasures I did share,
Plus all the many friends I had,
While I was going there.

How good it is that we have lived
And shared our lives and pleasures
With those we loved and cherished much—
These are life's greatest treasures.

Too bad the children of today
Can't learn the Golden Rule,
Along with English, Math, and Gym,
Taught in a One-Room School.

To Mandy

So many years I've waited,
All for this very day.
So many hours I've dreamed
Of just what I would say.
But, oh! the very sight of you
Standing there, no less,
Caused me to stop and panic;
Words I could not then express.
My lips were sealed, my eyes were damp,
A lump was in my throat—
I couldn't say the things I'd planned,
Or half the things I wrote.
Forgive me, dear, I'm now composed;
I'll tell you how I feel:
You're still the girl that I once knew,
Now that you're here for real.

To Vega (in Sweden)

I

It sure has been a long, long time,
Since you have gone away.
We miss you more and more, my dear,
At closing of each day.

We're glad the visit is so nice,
And Mother's feeling fine;
So tell her that we need you home,
And please come back on time.

Nenotska sends her love to you,
And says, "I miss you too."
She is waiting patiently,
As good dogs always do.

I'll be here when you arrive;
I'll meet you at the plane.
We hope this time you'll settle down,
And not leave us again.

II

Many miles across the sea,
A smiling someone, dear to me,
Enjoys home and family.

Talking o'er childhood dreams,
Seeing friends, ere long you've seen,
Good to be back home.

Mother, brothers, family,
Relatives and company,
All are there back home.

Soon again you'll fly once more,
Landing on this wondrous shore,
Where loved ones wait for you.

We count each and every day,
Since the time you went away,
Welcome, dear, back home.

III

Hope you're having loads of fun,
Meeting each and every one
You haven't seen for years.

Looking your own very best,
Day and night without much rest,
Having quite a ball.

Eating Swedish smorgasbords,
Dining out with Dukes and Lords,
Acting like a Queen.

Not a worry or a care,
Traveling freely here and there,
Enjoy it while you can.

Why I Love You

The little things you think to do,
The little things you say,
That little song you sing each morn,
Your kind and loving way.

The truthfulness you do impart,
Your dimpled Swedish smile—
All are things that I enjoy,
And make my life worthwhile.

To Vega

The mornings are a little brighter,
And birds sing sweeter too.
My heart is now a little lighter,
All because of you.

The flowers smell a little sweeter;
The grass is greener too,
For love has entered my poor heart,
And all because of you.

Love

Like sunshine filtering through a cloud,
I see your smiling face,
As freshness after summer's rain,
To feel your warm embrace.

The gracefulness of birds in flight,
When e'er I see you walk,
The melodies of angel harps,
When you begin to talk.

It seems that everything I see
Brings memories, dear, of you.
And life is now quite wonderful,
Because I love you true.

Each pebble on the wave-whipped beach,
Each tiny grain of sand,
Each star that twinkles in the sky,
All tell me that you're grand.

Cooled Love

I love you, dear, with all my heart,
And all my life and soul.
I'll always love you dearly,
Until the earth grows cold.
Each morning, I will love you,
Each evening, every night.
I'll love you on awakening
With ardor and delight.
And when the sun sinks in the west
I'll hold you close to me
And love you as I do today
And to eternity.

* * *

Now years have passed and love is cooled;
Each has gone his way.
Was this a passing fancy?
Why did we go astray?
What made our ardor wane and cool?
What caused that great mistake?
What caused the rift that brought divorce?
What wrong road did we take?
I was sincere and you were too;
We could not get along.
Each tried to boss the other one,
And that's when things went wrong.

A Fling

Within the realm of each man's heart,
There lies the urge to just be free
And taste the sins one reads about,
That they themselves might see.

To travel o'er the breadth and width
Of every foreign, mystic land,
Throwing caution to the wind,
Wealth and pleasures on command.

Sail the seas, the far-off realms,
A carefree life, just to pursue,
With no regrets to hold one back,
With nothing positive to do.

Then when he's had the run of things,
And age begins to show,
A rainbow suddenly appears,
Erasing age and aches and woe.

Deadly Game

To be loved is a pleasure;
To be wanted is a must.
To be sought after a fallacy,
To be caught is unjust.

Like a moth in the moonlight,
Drawn towards a candle flame,
Seeking only light and pleasure,
All too close, a deadly game.

The Beach

While strolling on the sandy beach,
Foamed waves lapping at my feet,
Sand crabs rushing here and there,
Shore birds winging through the air,
Balmy breezes fan my brow,
Ocean dampness in my hair,
Seashells with their shiny pearl,
Sudden gusts of sand awhirl,
Carefree in the morning sun,
Drinking deep at nature's trough,
Far from noise and din and strife—
This a truly happy life.

Grin and Bear It

Have you ever waited for your ship to come in,
Only to find you have waited in vain?
Have you ever bet on a horse just to win,
Yet you knew that you'd lose once again?
Have you ever put all of your eggs in one basket,
Then, too late, found the handle was bad?
Or met a new girl you were crazy about,
Then found that a husband she had?
Well, you are the guy that I'm talking about,
The guy who just sticks out his chin,
The guy who will gamble for the pleasure of it,
And suffers his loss with a grin.
You're one in a million; we need guys like you,
For you make life for others worthwhile.
The guy who can lose yet grin and bear it,
And still have a wonderful smile.

To My Friends

We gather here most every week
To further understand our feelings,
To share the love that's in our hearts,
And hear Poetic readings.

We've passed the crucial time of life;
No longer are we vain—
Our only hope, to spend these years,
In pleasantness less pain.

We relish memories of our past,
Our days of work, no longer needed.
Tho we have given our best years,
Our knowledge goes unheeded.

So now our thoughts and loves and woes,
We here will share together.
Let every day be filled with joy,
And sunshine be our weather.

Poetry

Poetry is beauty in the written word,
Raising the soul to boundless pleasure,
Uplifting the meek and mild,
Giving strength to the ill and aged,
Bringing love to a lonely heart,
And to the strong, a newfound treasure.

Autumn

It's autumn in the farmland,
Beautiful colors, hues, and tones.
We're sure that God is smiling,
And His love for us is shown.

Harvest labor is 'most over,
Cornstalks standing in the field.
Squash and pumpkins in the larder,
We're thankful for the gracious yield.

Peppers, onions from the rafters,
Spuds and yams are in the bin.
Apples, stored in bushel baskets,
What a harvest this has been!

Winter's snows are soon approaching,
Time to stock the kindling wood,
Time to seal the house from weather,
Time to stock the pantry good.

God, we thank You for this harvest,
And for all the things You've shared,
For the bounties You have given,
And the way You really cared.

Awaiting His Call

As I walk the path of live-alones,
A thought does comfort me,
For He who guides my every step
Will someday set me free.
He comforts every sorrowing day,
Although the road seems long,
For as I walk life's great pathway,
My heart is filled with song.
When e'er He bids me, I will come
To that great heavenly home,
For then I'll have companionship,
And never walk alone.

Church

'Twas Sunday morn, I 'rose at dawn,
    Got out my Sunday clothes.
Meticulously, I dressed that day,
    So careful what I chose.

The bells rang out at ten past ten;
    I drove, not to be late.
At twenty after, on the dot,
    I entered through the gate.

The greeters, standing at the door,
    All starched as they could be,
Each shook my hand—"Glad you could come,"
    And smiled so cheerfully.

The church was cool and dim and still,
    Light filtering through stained glass.
A feel of peace and reverence there,
    All worries seemed to pass.

A sudden hush fell on the crowd,
    Then anthems sweet and clear.
Angelic music, raised in song,
    Came floating to my ear.

The sermon, on that Sunday morn,
    Was "Meet God Face to Face."
And now that I look back once more,
    Those words I did embrace.

Now in my waning years of life,
    That message lingers still,
How He laid down his life for me,
    That day on Calvary Hill.

Old Age

At this ripe old age,
Values aren't the same
As when one's young and foolish.
The years and time
Smooth off the edge,
And leave us mild and droolish.

Of course we feel,
That due to years
And hard-knock education,
We think we are
Entitled to
A lot of dedication.

Age gives us guts
To stand our ground,
Demanding what we crave.
We raise a fuss,
And rant and cuss;
We're old but we are brave.

Some things we do
Seem strange, it's true,
But that's the fun of living.
We like to throw
Our weight around,
Yet we are most forgiving.

If someone really needs a friend,
Or just someone to care,
Please look us up;
Tell us your woes—
We'll join you in despair.

No matter what
We say or do,
There's much love in our heart.
We may act tough,
Or seem quite gruff—
That's just the outward part.

An Ode to a Timeworn Heart

Old timeworn Heart,
I'll call on you once more.
You'll feel the strain and agony,
When love comes in your door.
Much faster, you will beat again;
The wear and tear will burden you.
A tower of strength, you've served me well
In past loves that we knew.
Pour out your goodness once again,
To pleasures, joy, and beauty.
May your reward be Faithfulness
In this last honored duty.

Glendora

At the base of the mighty San Gabriels,
In the shadow of Baldy's grand spire,
Where the orange and the lemon waft fragrant,
The heart of the citrus empire.

A jewel in emerald surroundings,
Dainty—Lovely—Serene,
Progressive, yet friendly and homey,
A figment of everyone's dream.

Flowers of every description
Abound in that rich fertile soil.
Jacaranda, Eucalyptus, Bougainvillea
Crown our city so royal.

Churches of all denominations,
Schools of the highest degree,
Citrus College with all of its splendor,
City Hall, quaint and grand as can be.

Homes of grandeur, livable mansions,
Apartments with every detail,
Hospitals, staffed and ready with experts,
Shops and markets to hold your appeal.

This is our town as we know it,
Beautiful, Bountiful Glendora,
Rich in the legends of folklore,
Yet modern as only tomorrow.

The Foothills

Though not a native of this state,
I now call it my home.
Who could resist the beauty here,
No matter where you roam?
If all the folks could ever see
What this land has to give,
I'm sure they all would be right here,
And here they'd always live.
The fertile lands so rich and green,
The groves of citrus trees,
Where Palm and Eucalyptus grow
In perfect harmony.
This valley is a paradise,
A place to play or rest.
With all its great advantages,
You're bound to feel your best.
The tall San Gabriels to the north,
So graceful, rugged, grand,
The snow-capped peaks and Baldy,
A winter wonderland.
Baseball, golf, and racing,
Swimming in the sea,
Fishing, boating, skiing,
A friendly place to be.
Barbecues the whole year round,
Bathing in the sun,
A patio with every home,
To rest when day is done.
You cannot beat this magic land,
For everything is here—
One visit and you're sure to stay,
Enjoying each and every year.
I dedicate these words of praise,
And all they do entail,
To this great Valley that I love—
The old San Gabriel.

The San Gabriel Valley Symphony

The San Gabriel Valley Symphony
Extends to you this call
To hear the strains of artists grand,
Great works of one and all.

To hear the haunting melodies,
The rhythm and the chords—
To drink of beauty genius gave
More beautiful than words.

The sweetness of each violin
Most takes your breath away;
The oboe and the low woodwinds
Bring feelings of dismay.

French horns and harps, gifts of the gods,
Elate your very soul.
The beat of drums and cymbals clash—
A climax to it all.

You owe yourself this luxury,
Brilliantly brought to you,
For love of Art is yours alone
To enjoy your whole life through.

Memories

Remember back to yesterday
When you were in your teens.
Think of things you once did do
And felt they were not wrong.
You were not bad, or so you thought;
Rebellion then was strong.

You wanted only what was fair,
Not to be pushed around.
You wanted recognition then,
A chance to just be heard,
To be an equal with the rest,
And not to be interred.

And so today another group,
Teenage boys and girls,
Speak out and do some "kooky" things
That they might then be known.
Give them a chance to speak their piece;
Their wisdom will be shown.

Year after year, till end of time,
This problem we will face,
Unless we try to understand.
Give the teens their rightful place;
Let them voice their thoughts today
To save us from disgrace.

Each twenty years another war
When thousands meet their doom,
Famine killing thousands more,
Millionaires yet poverty—
A frightful outlook for our teens—
It's time we listened to their plea.

Stress

In times of stress, we never know
The feelings stirred within our hearts.
Reactions sometimes turn to hate,
Bitter words, violent fate.

Other times we stop to think,
Carefully weighing every thought.
Reactions are quite calm and cool;
Reason then becomes our tool.

Is God Dead?

We ask the question, "Is God dead?"
Or did He leave that tomb?
Could He be here among us now,
To judge us at our doom?

Is He a part of every plan,
A guide of every thought?
I feel that this could not be true,
Yet this is what we're taught.

Corruption in its greatest form
Surrounds us every day.
Evil seems to be our goal;
We sin in every way.

On bended knees, we ask His help;
Most all admit some faith.
Some even try to live as He;
Some try to take His place.

If "God is dead," as some believe,
Did He then die in vain?
And all His sufferings were for naught,
As well as all His pain?

Today I'm Sixty

When I look back on sixty years
And all the things I've done,
And weigh them for both good and bad,
I'm sure the good has won.

I've always tried to give my best
In every way I knew.
The underdog was my first choice,
In hopes he would come through.

I've often strained myself a bit,
To give my friends a break,
And many times picked up the check
That someone else should take.

Though modest is my wealth today,
I'm blessed with conscience clear.
And when I go to bed at night,
I have no thought of fear.

I'm blessed with health, a pleasant job,
A happy home is mine.
What more could anyone desire,
In sixty years of time?

Announcement

The Palace was gay on that August eve,
Happy the guests and the hosts,
Radiant the Bride and Groom to be,
As they drank Champagne to a toast.

Two youthful lovers, so much in love,
Willing to give and to share,
Two happy people, soon to be wed,
Announcing their betrothal there.

Soon to be sharing their pleasures as one,
Fulfilling a long-awaited dream,
May each new day bring a joy never known;
May each thought be filled with esteem.

As you journey through life some shadows appear,
Causing some worry and pain.
Keep always in mind, you're Husband and Wife,
And true love brings sunshine again.

Our Baby

Someday I'll have a little girl,
And she'll look just like me;
I'll dress her in the finest clothes
For everyone to see.

And all the love that's in my heart
I'm going to share each day,
For she will be my little girl,
Like me in every way.

Of course, if fate brings us a boy
He'll be his daddy's pal,
But I will share him just the same,
At least for just a while.

He'll be the image of his dad
And do the things dads like;
I'm sure we'll both be proud of him—
Our rugged little tyke.

Spring

A touch of warmth is in the air,
Grasses green, most everywhere.
Birds sing sweetly in the trees,
The smell of freshness in the breeze,
For spring has come.

Students on their way to school,
In the fields the newborn foal,
Occasionally a flower is seen,
Along the rushing mountain stream,
For spring has come.

Life takes on a new aspect,
Coats of paint where once neglect,
Colors gay most everywhere;
Laughter seems to fill the air,
For spring has come.

Milestones

Many, many years ago, when I was just a boy,
I loved to roam the countryside
To see the beauty there,
To walk beneath the chestnut trees and gather
    nuts galore,
Or track the flight of honeybees and take what
    was in store,
Or climb a mountain to the top, and view land
    far and wide,
Or stretch out on a sun-kissed rock or sleep on
    beds of pine,
Or wade a rushing mountain stream of water
    clear and cold,
Or stand and breathe the fresh clean air or
    pan for flakes of gold,
Or watch the birds soar on the wind or chipmunks
    hard at play,
Or hear the call of wolves at night or roosters
    call for day.
That was a happy time of life,
But now I'm old and gray.
I'll always cherish those good times for still
    another day.

Endearments

December 26

Too bad your birthday comes this time,
With all the holidays.
I guess it cuts down on the gifts
And fun in many ways.

So why don't you just change the date,
'Cause none will e'er surmise,
And say your birthday's in July?
'Twill be a big surprise!

Then everyone will send a gift,
And there'll be parties too,
And who will know just when it is,
Except your mom and you?

A Safe Flight Home

When I looked up at the stars tonight
And saw how bright they shone
I knew that brightness was for you
To light your way back home.

Each twinkle seemed to say to me,
"Don't worry, she'll be all right,
For we'll watch over her for you,
While she is on this flight."

A Bedtime Story

Close your eyes now, sunny boy,
For you will need your rest.
Tomorrow morning Santa comes,
And you must feel your best.

When you look up and see a star
That twinkles merrily,
It means that Santa's on his way
To visit you and me.

So close your eyes and get your sleep;
Tomorrow soon will be.
When you awake, you'll find new toys
Beneath a Christmas tree.

Lyn

I am a little girl of two,
Quite pretty but so shy.
And I can do most anything,
If I but wish to try.

I'm daddy's little angel
And mommy's little dear;
Granddad calls me Princess,
So I have naught to fear.

When I am just a little bad,
And daddy says he'll "spank,"
I simply have to roll my eyes,
Then it becomes a prank.

It's hard to fool my mommy,
'Cause we're together more,
So I just give her one big hug
And even up the score.

When dad and mommy take me out
To visit friends or places,
I am the charmer of the crowd,
Displaying my best graces.

They are so very proud of me
And tell me every day,
But even though I'm only two
I sure do get my way.

Your Son

Who gives you more pleasure, when brought to this
   world,
Who shows you more love and devotion?
Who seeks your advice, when problems arise,
Who causes so little commotion?

Who holds to your hand or sits on your lap,
Who tells you the great things he's done?
Who makes you so proud, when you brag to your
   friends,
Who else could it be than a SON?

Happy Birthday, Son

Did not have time to buy a card;
Sure hope that this will do,
For, after all, it's not the card—
It's what I think of you.

No greater son hath any man,
No prouder dad than me.
You're all that anyone could want,
Or anyone could be.

The Astronauts

We have a rendezvous up there among
    the stars,
In that vast outer space so far.
Out there in tranquil skies, we'll set
    our course,
And all celestial bodies will rejoice.

We'll tell the moon and stars and
    Venus, too,
Of all the plans that Earth expects to do.
And from our orbit, we'll look down
    at you,
For we are just space travelers passing
    through.

From One Republican to Another

Though your man lost this election,
Do not let it get you down.
Losing now is no reflection—
Nixon still will be around.

In four years you'll feel elated,
When the country's gone to hell,
And the things their platform stated
Have been shelved, or really smell.

Try and be a graceful loser;
Let them not see how you feel.
Remember you were not the chooser
Of the man that won the deal.

Utopia

Wouldn't it be wonderful, if everything went fine,
And nothing ever bothered you, and you had loads of time?
And every morn when you arose, you had no job to do,
Yet, when the weekend rolled around, a check was given you?
And every wish you ever had was granted just like that,
Or you could go most anywhere, in next to nothing flat?
Well, that is called Utopia, at least that's what they say;
The only hitch to having it—it vanished yesterday.

Complaints

We think our taxes are too high,
And schools take too much land,
And always at election time
Bond issues are the trend.

We all complain of lack of rain,
Yet, when the rains do come,
We're still not wholly satisfied,
For it cuts down our fun.

Transportation causes grief,
So two cars are the rule,
And Sonny also needs a car,
When he goes off to school.

The price of food seems rather high,
When to the store we go,
Yet we don't count the work involved,
That helps to make it so.

We all demand the highest wage,
Fringe benefits galore,
And still complain of income tax,
And wish there was no more.

Some folks are never satisfied
And never seem quite calm,
Yet would they trade this life at home
For one in Vietnam?

The Pirates

Sailor tales and sailor tunes,
Ships, Islands, and Doubloons,
And Pirates and buried gold.
Of Blackbeard, Flint, and other Kings,
Who plundered many towns and ships,
Taking wine and gold and things,
Giving Men-o'-War the slip.
The Jolly Roger was their flag,
And from the mast it flew,
A warning to all merchant ships
That their proud days were through.
With cutlass hanging at their sides,
Pistols at their waist,
A colored cloth around their head,
A fearful sight to face.
With sails unfurled, all hands on deck,
And cannons fully primed,
They bore down on unwary foes,
Each boarding rightly timed.
Screaming, swearing, savage brutes,
Their onslaught filled with hate,
Overpowering all who did resist,
Surrender came too late.
Flint buried treasure on Treasure Isle,
A place far out at sea.
And there he left his dangerous men,
The ones that mutiny.
He paid his score by dying,
And Blackbeard by being hung.
And all their vast ill-gotten gains
Have benefited none.

Christmas

Glad Christmas comes just once a year,
With its gaiety and joys,
And jingle bells and merry songs,
And happy girls and boys.

With traffic hazards at their worst,
And prices at their peak,
Poor worn-out Dad and Mother, too,
Too tired to hardly speak.

With lavish gifts and Christmas cards,
And feasts fit for a King,
Open houses, gadding sprees,
While church and sleigh bells ring.

Sporting games and big parades,
A happy day for all,
While relatives and friends drop in,
To pay their yearly call.

Though Christ was born on Christmas Day,
So many years ago,
Guess He would wonder, were He here,
How we could change it so.

A Christmas to Remember

It was Christmas Day not long ago,
The old tin palace all aglow.
A festive spirit filled the air;
Family and friends were gathered there—
Napkin Angels overhead,
Golden balls on golden thread,
Dickens characters on display,
A Christmas tree so bright and gay.

Businessmen, their duties through,
Housewives, writers, clergy too,
Babes in arms, and aged folks,
Singing carols, telling jokes,
Travelers from across the sea,
All in perfect harmony,
Joining hands in silent prayer—
Christ was ever present there.

Toasts were made, mere words to tell,
The greatest hostess, knowing well,
How thankful we were asked to be,
A part of her own family—
Ham and turkey, for the treats,
Peas, creamed onions, candied sweets,
Pumpkin pie, and fruitcake too,
Coffee when the meal was through.

A joyous day, a happy day,
The warmth and friendship long will stay,
For in each heart there lingers still,
The thought of Christ on Calvary Hill,
Who gave His all that we might share,
The closeness that we felt while there.
Now as we go our separate ways,
We'll long remember Christmas Day.

A Christmas Thought

It's getting round that time of year,
When smiles come out and friends appear.
No matter how you really feel,
You'll make your laughter seem quite real.

Merry Christmas, everyone,
Vacations, parties, loads of fun,
Presents, clothing, eating sprees,
Gatherings round the Christmas trees.

Yet seldom do we turn our head
To heed the one true thought, inbred,
For Christ was born on Christmas Day.
And we, down on our knees, should pray.

Goodwill to all should last all year,
Then that would be true Christmas cheer.

My Thrill

Of all the things that I have done,
Some good and some quite bad,
I think the greatest thrill of all
Came when I was a lad.

My folks and I set out by car
To visit relatives;
Unknowingly we met some friends—
This was the thrill I live.

We crossed the old Ohio line,
The limestone roads, with dust
Obliterating all we passed,
To stay ahead a must.

A Klaxon sounded close behind;
A road race then ensued,
Each driver giving all he had
To try and stay pursued.

Finally we could not endure
The pressure brought to bear
And took our licking like a man,
Dust settling everywhere.

We followed at a distant pace,
Composing as we could;
The limestone dust had left its mark,
As well we knew it would.

In Marion at the obelisk
We parked beside the car
That gave us such a thrilling race
And then learned who they were.

Henry Ford sat in the front;
A tall, thin man was he.
He was the first to shake our hands
With much hilarity.

The rear seat held two famous men,
Firestone and Edison.
They also shook our hands and laughed,
So glad that they had won.

The reason for their being there—
It pains me much to tell—
President Harding passed away,
This day his funeral.

Long years passed by; I'm now a man
And have a year-old son.
Vacation time is here for us,
Chataqua and the fun.

One day while strolling to the beach,
My son held in my arms,
A lady stopped me and explained,
"Your handsome son has charm."

This lady asked if she might share
Her early-morning rides,
If my son, Bill, would go along
To beach and countryside.

She also asked if I would spend
A little time each day
In talking to Tom Edison,
Who now was old and gray.

And so, my friends, I too am old,
But memories linger yet,
The thrill of meeting those great men,
A thrill I'll ne'er forget.